And It Was Told

of a

Certain Potter

Walter C. Lanyon

Author of "Embers"—"Abd Allah, Teacher, Healer"
—"Know Thyself"—"Face to Face"—"Once upon a
Time" and "Run Out Doors and Look Up".

Contents

Published by
Book & Art Shop
414 Merrill Bldg.
Milwaukee, Wis

Abd Allah, the Potter

AND the sun streaming in through the eastern window awakened Abd Allah, the potter. He stretched his lithe, muscular body luxuriously and, rubbing his eyes, sat up. The boy Jethro lay wrapped in slumber, his harp close at hand.

"Jethro, Jethro," called Abd Allah, " 'tis morn! Get thee to the well and fetch up the water for the morning meal."

Jethro got sleepily into his picturesque costume of crimson with its heavy blue silken sash. He was a happy type of youth, a true son of the orient, his skin the color of copper and his raven locks matted in curls to his well-shaped head. Some years before Abd Allah had found him begging in the streets of Jerusalem, and had taken him home. Of his early life little was known, save that at one time he lived on a boat which sailed the Nile. And it was upon this boat that an old sailor had taught him to play the harp. His voice, which was natural and clear, had a warmth of expression seldom found in an untrained singer.

Pushing aside the heavy curtain of woolen stuff that covered the doorway of their abode, Abd Allah stepped into the outer court and raised his eyes to the eastern heavens. It was a new day and the sky was a mass of gold and crimson, shot

9

with the palest mauve. "The heavens declare the glory of God; and the firmament sheweth His handiwork," breathed Abd Allah. There was a thrill in his voice as he repeated it; he felt the impetus of the new day creeping over him and thus he reasoned:

It is a new day, fresh from the hands of God, and I am a new man (idea) fresh from the hands of God. I have but the glowing, ever-present now, which is pregnant with opportunity and goodness. And as this day cannot look back into yesterday, neither can I bring from yesterday any of its storms or sorrows. And as every flower that blooms and every bird that goes singing through the long hours are new and fresh acquaintances to the day, so every man that I meet shall be new and good to me, a friend and brother.

As he stood filling his soul full of the morning and the glories of the new day, a single bird winged his way into the liquid blue, shrilling his wild song of joy. It was almost as if his thoughts had taken the "Wings of the morning." And as he was thus setting his house (mind) in order for the day, Jethro came through the large open gateway with the jar of water on his head. He, too, had been drinking in the wonders of the heavens, and, setting the jar down, he stood beside Abd Allah and said:

"Look across that silver sea of olive trees, there in the valley of the Mount! See how she stands wrapped in that bluish mist! Is it not beautiful,

Father Abd Allah? And see how the great leaves of those yellow-green banana trees sway in the breeze. The fragrance of a thousand wild vines and flowers fills the air. Is it not a wonderful world, and are we not rich, Father Abd, to have this picture ever before us?"

And Abd Allah answered: "Praise be unto God whose handiwork is shown."

* * * *

Now, Abd Allah was a potter by trade, and he worked into the color of his vases the glories of the heavens and of nature, and into his designs he painted wonderful lessons of gratitude and peace. He was also a letter writer, and in short, a sort of confessor or judge, inasmuch as those in trouble came to him with their problems for solution, and he always sent them away satisfied and with new courage. And, lastly, Abd Allah, which means servant of God, was a true servant of the Most High.

Of friends Abd Allah had many, and these he found among all classes, from the lordly nobleman, in his wonderful palace of snowy marble, to the humble herdsman, who dwelt without the city gates. In short he had a breadth of love that reached out to all men.

His dwelling, which contained two small rooms, was in an enclosed court and faced the east. In front of it stood a thick, bushy almond tree, and it was under the shade of this tree that Abd sat day after day working at his vases, or

writing letters, with Jethro close at hand to sing
to Abd and play on his harp. A glance at the
open doorway, with naught but a heavy, oriental
curtain, immediately bespoke the moral courage
of the man Abd, and his open, God-fearing nature, for his dwelling was located in the outskirts
of Jerusalem, near one of the less frequented of
its seven gates, and many considered it unsafe
to leave their doors and windows unbarred
against thieves.

And oft-times, as he worked, Abd Allah told
Jethro the story of his vase, and sometimes, per-
chance he was starting a new vase, he would
work into it the solution of the problem of some
troubled one, who had come burdened with too
much care.

Abd Allah had learned, years before, that as
a pebble thrown into a pool of water brings one
ring after another to the surface until they reach
the outer edge, so one good thought dropped into
the stagnant mind will bring ring after ring of
thought to the surface, until the whole mind has
been stirred; and he likewise knew that by dropping these thoughts into the pool of a dormant or
sick mind, at last, when enough have been
dropped into its depths, it will rise and flow off
in a tiny stream, and by flowing (becoming active) purify itself, and, not only thereby receive
a blessing, but water field and forest and prove
a benefit to mankind. And though it had been
unloved and shunned as a stagnant pool, little
children may wade in its cool depths and scatter
flowers on its surface.

"Love is the only active element of the Universe," Abd had told Jethro. "Be sure you are filled with Love all the while; let naught else into your consciousness, and as you go you will reflect it in some way that 'will draw all men unto you'." So Jethro reflected Love through song and music, and Abd Allah through his pottery and his well-modulated, sonorous voicings of Truth. But there are many modes of letting your light so shine before men that they will call you blessed.

Prayer

T was the hour of prayer in the city of Jerusalem. About the gate where Abd Allah and Jethro were stationed many of the merchants and loiterers were kneeling and calling upon the name of their God to succor and help them. The little band about Abd Allah stood listening in silence to the mumblings of the men at prayer. "Tell us something of true prayer, Abd Allah," said one of the men standing near him; "something of that for which this outward expression stands."

"We admit," Abd Allah began, "that God is good, that He is All, that He is everywhere, and the cause and effect of all that really exists. We acknowledge Him to be the source from which every good gift comes.

"Further, in the line of common reasoning, we know that prayer in its generally accepted sense means desire. This being the case, we begin to see that our very desires or prayers, in so far as they are good, proceed from God, and are not as we formerly supposed self-originated requests or petitions, but rather the urge of God (good) endeavoring to find expression in us, good endeavoring to be made manifest in the flesh.

"Perhaps, for example, you are praying for health. You are desiring it, but as God is the only creator and good, in reality your desire for

15

health is but the will of God trying to express itself through you. 'God is willing to do exceeding abundantly, more than we ask or think.' God is 'willing' it. And as your desire for health is prompted by His willingness to be expressed in perfect strength, you reverse the proposition and find that, in reality, the health and strength of God, good, are seeking to find expression in you; not you seeking to bring them into your thought.

"If you are praying for supply, is it not in reality God's fullness seeking further expression in you? Is it not the 'still small voice' calling for a greater expression of substance, God? God is all substance; then the desire for supply is a greater desire for God, or God endeavoring to manifest Himself more fully. And suddenly you turn from your prayers of beseeching to the attitude of 'Speak, for thy Servant heareth', and 'Not my will but thine be done.' You begin endeavoring to find out what His wishes are

"Then our part in prayer, after we have acclaimed God as all and ever-present good, is to relax, to let go and step aside; literally and figuratively to say 'Glorify thy Son that thy son may also glorify thee;' that is, make thyself manifest in me, fulfill thy desires. Fling open wide the portals of your mind and bid Him enter who waits without; make thyself wholly acceptable to Him, to use for His good pleasure, and your desires and prayers will find their rightful expression.

"Having given yourself over to His expression, see that no selfishness enters and tries to hoard

16

up His expression of Love as it passes through you You are merely a channel, a steward placed in charge of the gift, a caretaker, but not an owner. Use freely His Love as you do the air about you, but see that nothing clogs the channel of expression to others.

"Now if God is love and everywhere present, then we live in an atmosphere of Love for 'in Him we live, and move, and have our being.' Let us establish a better sense of this Atmosphere of Love in which we constantly move First, it is unchangeable and all powerful, and you are completely submerged in it and must of necessity be governed by it. As a fish is completely submerged in water, so man is submerged, surrounded by mind, and as the fish of the sea finds his supply, health and happiness in the medium of water, so man must be fed, clothed and cared for by the One Mind or Atmosphere of Love that completely envelops him. In fact, in establishing a fuller and better knowledge of this Atmosphere of Love, we lose sight of ourselves completely, and thus in losing sight of self we have stepped aside and a complete healing, regeneration, or expression of Love has taken place, a full expression of His love has been made manifest in the flesh.

"It is quite as impossible for man to reflect only a part of the qualities of mind, or of this Atmosphere of Love in which he lives and moves, as it is for a fish to be partly dry and yet remain submerged in the ocean If man reflects one of the qualities of mind he must reflect them all.

If he reflects life, he must also reflect supply, health, happiness and success. He cannot move into a place where any of these qualities are wanting—there are no desert places in eternal mind—any more than a fish could swim into a dry spot in the ocean.

"Comes now our impersonal work, both for ourselves and others. As we establish a better idea of God as ever-present Love and fix our attention on this one quality, we unconsciously help ourselves and also anyone upon whom our thoughts may rest, because if we are submerged in Love nothing of an opposite nature can enter or affect us, and we partake of the qualities of this atmosphere just as the fish is naturally wet, not through any effort on his part; he does not try to be wet, he just is. When we come to the point that we can consciously feel that we are living in this Atmosphere of Love, we cannot help reflecting the qualities of it. We are one with God, for we are 'image and likeness,' and what shall separate us from the Love that He bestows?"

The Perfect Man

EARLY on the morning of market day Abd Allah arose and awakened Jethro. June was yet young and hovered over the distant hills with an enchanting freshness. A million diamond dew drops caught and held the sun a prisoner, reflecting the mysteries of the rainbow. Out over the valley, which was lavishly dotted with flowers and trees, a transparent purple mist foretold the coming day. Abd Allah was happy. He felt the thrill that only a mind filled with goodness can feel on the contemplation of the beautiful. Life was so worth-while; there was so much good to be had for the mere reaching out; there was a constant tonic of youth and health to be drunk from the wonders of nature.

After breakfast he and Jethro started toward the east gate with their small load of vases.

"Does not the morning, with its mystery, thrill you?" he said to Jethro, and without waiting for an answer he continued, filling his lungs with the fine morning air: "It is good to be alive. It is good to know that you are a perfect man, made in His image and likeness."

"A perfect man?" questioned Jethro. "Just look, Father Abd, who comes there," and as Abd looked he saw Jaraj, the herder. He was surely a pitiful looking piece of humanity, quite bent over and in ill health. "Is he, too, a perfect man?" asked Jethro as they passed on their way.

They walked on in silence for a while and Abd Allah said:

"Jethro, you speak some Greek, a little Egyptian and Arabic, and in all these languages they have a different symbol for the same numbers That is, you can give expression to the quantity two in as many different tongues as you know, and while the material symbol in each instance will differ, the quantity remains the same. It is eternally two, and if every symbol that was used to express two were swept away, the quantity two would remain just the same Age will not add to it nor take from it. This is essentially true of all realities. So is it with the perfect man, made in His image and likeness: the substance of him is perfect and good and cannot change though the material symbol that represents him may be anything from a hunch-back to an athlete

"Further, Jethro, when you see a column of figures, some perfectly drawn and others poorly made, do you stop for a minute and say: 'That two is poorly made; I cannot give it the full value of two?' No. You give it the full value without ever a thought of taking from it or adding to it because it is larger than the rest. In your mind it has a fixed value or substance and that is what you give it, no matter what the symbol looks like. Then is it not our duty to give to the material symbol of man his full inheritance, that of perfection and goodness, and to look beyond the material symbol, just as you do in figures, and reckon the absolute quantity and substance of Màn made in His image and likeness?

20

"What use would men have for criticism if they had this fact firmly established in their minds? And what a wonderful help and stimulus the world would receive again, to know that every man is perfect, just as he was created."

"Then criticism is really 'bearing false witness' against thy brother, is it not?" said Jethro, "and what other motive could prompt bearing false witness against a man than hate?"

"Yes," said Abd Allah, "Criticism is hate, and with hate in our minds love cannot enter nor abide."

"But another good point to me," said Abd Allah, as they walked along, "is that while the material symbol for man may appear distorted, with the right thought and love he can be made straight and healed of his infirmities. Think of the symbol of the perfect man who lay at the pool of Bethesda for thirty and eight years, and how all that time he was unable to help himself. Is it not appalling to note the lack of right thinking on his part. There he lay, a son of the All Powerful, an 'image and likeness', governed by the one omnipresent, omnipotent law of good, unable to move himself. And all the while the men at the court were giving him the lie, and refusing to count him as a perfect man, until one day Jesus came by and saw him as a perfect man, with the result that the thirty and eight years of bondage disappeared and the man came into his heritage of dominion.

"What disease or evil condition can present itself as permanent when we stop for a minute to realize that we are perfect, created so by God and sustained eternally by Him?

"Was it not through Daniel's realization of the indestructible qualities of the perfect man that he escaped the jaws of the lions? He put their laws of matter to naught by knowing that the perfect man was indestructible.

"But it is necessary that we do more than declare this truth of perfection; having 'done all, to stand,' stay put: we see that though Daniel proved the powerlessness of the lions immediately he entered the den, yet he had to remain (stand) there all night 'Patience must have her perfect work'."

Abd Allah's Philosophy

"AWAKE thou that sleepeth;" get some of the now-ness into your thinking. Don't wait to die to get into heaven; "Behold the kingdom of Heaven is at hand;" it is within you.

What is heaven? It is happiness and joy; it is right thinking and right acting. It is making obstacles stepping stones instead of stumbling blocks. It is getting plenty of blue sky and sunshine into your mind.

All about you lie infinite possibilities. Opportunity and fortune literally plead with you to take them in. Fate is the blind belief of the fearful; it is the great excuse for failure and stagnation. Failure is the letting go of your grip. There is no such a word as failure to the right thinking man. True, material conditions may change, but with the destruction of the shell of an egg we have an advanced state of progress, that will eventually fly off into the great free sky, thrilling with joy.

Failure to the material sense may be opportunity and fortune forcing you to make a step forward that you have heretofore been reluctant to take. Don't lose heart because you are down and out. You can always start over; there is always a new day. Success is not measured in dollars and cents; it is measured in happiness and con-

tentment. Happiness is not an elusive something
that keeps dodging you, but a permanent state to
the right thinking man. Have some of the qualities of a cork; refuse to stay under.

Get plenty of joy into your thinking. Try
singing instead of mourning. Try realizing what
it is to be a son of the Most High, a son of the
King. Get some of the nobility that is yours into
your thought. Be noble.

Protect yourself by keeping your thought filled
with goodness and truth; if it is full of good
there is no room left for evil or fear. Evil thinking is the plague that produces all sickness, sin
and death; and right thinking corrects this. You
cannot think death and life at the same time;
either one or the other holds the floor. Neither
can you think riches and poverty, health and sickness. Be sure then that you are thinking on the
right side. When you are thinking right, no
plague shall come nigh thy dwelling.

Have you lost your material home? Then you
are now ready to enter into your divine estate,
and as the synonym for home is happiness (not
house), and happiness is a state of mind, you find
yourself already established in your new abode,
which is filled with large courts wherein you may
walk in peace. This kind of home is "under the
shadow of His mighty wing." The losing of a
material home is like the dropping off of the coty-
ledons of a tiny plant. The plant has lost nothing in parting with these impediments; but is free
and ready to grow heavenward.

Have you lost your best friend; did he betray you? This may help you to know that to lean on your own understanding is a dangerous thing, and further that God is the only true friend of man; that He is unchangeable and eternal; neither does He call for special favors, loans, etc., but only for fair thinking about Him.

Have you lost your fortune? All substance is His, and the fact that you are His perfect child gives you ample supply. He is responsible for your sustenance; you can of yourself do nothing. You did not ask to come here; He placed you here and He will provide. He is able to do all things, and to prepare a table before you in the presence of your enemies (in the presence of want). Plant your grain of mustard seed (faith) and watch it move mountains (doubts and fears).

When you act, act as one having authority. Put on the full armor of God. Don't imagine that because you have a sword in your hand you are safe. Put on the Helmet of right thinking, the Breastplate of righteousness. Be "shod with the preparation of the gospel." Have your shield engraved with the words, "Who is so great a God as our God?" Then your two-egded sword of wisdom will cut through the enemy's lines.

"Patience must have her perfect work." Remember that it takes repeated good thoughts to be effective. One good, strong thought, offset by the rest of the day spent in evil thinking, will not accomplish results for good Remember that the walls of Jerico did not fall down the first time they were encircled; but the Israelites did not give up, knowing that when enough good thoughts were directed against those walls, they would crumble away, and they did.

Do you suffer because your grandfather ate sour grapes? He is the one that should have suffered for that, and not you. You, probably, out of your own good wisdom, would have selected sweet grapes. Don't let the stupid law of heredity bind you; put it to flight with the powerful command, "Call no man your father, save God." What belief of inherited sin or sickness can withstand this?

Rejoice and be exceeding glad, for all things are possible to the man who puts his trust absolutely in God, and who knows that with Him all things are possible here and now.

The Man Who Resisted

ONCE more the sturdy almond tree had covered itself with a sheet of snowy-white
blossoms, and once more the caressing
breath of spring had wooed each blossom
and lured it from its resting place. One by one
they had launched out from the parent branch
and floated in a zig-zag course to the ground.
Unconsciously the unfoldment of life goes on
from one stage to another, and the almond tree,
which only a short time ago stood a silvery mass
of loveliness, under the sapphire dome of the
heavens, caught a mellow tint of autumn, and
again the ever active, ceaseless progress of life
lured, one by one, the yellow leaves from the tree.

Out over the land, autumn had painted with a
lavish hand. Here a dash of deep purple and
there a bank of gold. The distant foot-hills rose
like tongues of flame against the deep blue of the
sky. Here and there was a deep green tree which
had not yet been nipped by the frost, and again
in the distance could be seen the delicately etched
branches of trees already bare.

There was a mellowness in the air; a dreamy
wistfulness that caused one to sit and wonder,
to sit and dream. And it was on this day that
Abd Allah sat pondering and dreaming over the
wonders of life.

At length he resumed his work. "Come hither
Jethro," he called to the boy. "Bring your harp,

for I would have you sing to me; sing and play to me that I may mold some of this mystic beauty of the autumn into my vase, that in years to come someone gazing on it may take hope again."

"What is hope?" said Jethro, for he was fond of hearing Abd Allah explain the abstract. "Hope," said Abd, "is the red bird singing of spring on the bleak February bough; it is the spark of light which the traveler sees at the other end of the 'slough of despond,' it is the early spring lily peeping through the snow. But I would listen to thee a while. What will you sing to me?"

So Jethro, taking his harp, began:

The wheel of the potter turns round and round,
    Shaping his various wares.
Some to hold water and some to hold wine,
    Some to hold flowers fair.
Into each vessel the potter will mold
    True thoughts of usefulness,
And thus will the thought of the potter live,
    Ever waiting to bless.

    God is the potter and man is the clay.
        He works out his infinite plan.
    Each idea has a mission to fill,
        For each is a perfect man.

At this point in his song Jethro was interrupted by the loud shouting of someone at the gate. Laying aside his harp he ran across the court and gazed out. "It is Haasn and his mule," he called back to Abd Allah, "coming over the hill. He is staggering, drunk on new wine."

"Poor Haasn," said Abd Allah; "he is the man who resisted."

"Resisted," said Jethro. "What do you mean, Father Abd Allah? Is he not at this moment in the power of his worst enemy—wine? And has he not repeatedly fought against it to no avail?"

"Yes," said Abd, "and in constantly resisting the temptation to drink has he not made it something real, a personal devil which has absolute power over him? Do not the sacred scrolls teach 'resist not?' Man is superior to matter and its laws, for he is 'image and likeness.' He is not bidden to obey every whim of the mortal senses. He has been given dominion and sonship. God is Law; and did not Christ Jesus come to 'fulfill the law,' not the laws, and the law that he came to fulfill was the law of dominion; and did he not say The works that I do ye shall do also, and even greater?

"Remember the story of Jacob; how he struggled (resisted) all night (in ignorance) and that when the morning light came (truth and light) he loosed the lie (stopped resisting it) and let it go Is it not worth while to note that Jacob 'let it go?' That which he had resisted and struggled with all night, and which had caused him to suffer he merely had to 'let go.' So it is with all material law. We hold to it; it cannot cling to us for there is nothing to support it And when I see a man struggling with a belief of sin or sickness I am reminded of a child holding a wild animal with one hand and fighting it with the other and then crying because it hurts him, instead of letting go of it.

"In the case of Jacob we know not what the problem was, but let us suppose it was the temptation to drink that was causing him to resist and fight all night, and suddenly it dawned upon his consciousness 'Ye do not need to fight ...set yourself.. see the salvation of the Lord;' 'The battle is not yours, but the Lord's. And then the whispered pass word, which will lead you safely through all evil, 'Speak as one having authority,' and 'Dominion over all things' Would he, do you suppose, keep on fighting his temptation? Rather would he not suddenly find himself superior to the whole situation?

"If you resist a thing, you fear it, and if you fear it you necessarily endow it with power to hurt you. For who would resist anything that he was not afraid of? We are not afraid of so-called powerless things

"Meet every problem that comes to you as its master, knowing that God is working with you and that to be of one mind with Him is to be in the majority, for God is all powerful. The Hebrew children knew what it meant to be at one with God, and obeyed His Law instead of the laws of matter, with a result that the flames, which consumed others, left them untouched.

"It took only a pebble (right thought) to slay

Goliath, who had become real and terrible through material thinking and reasoning, and through resistance.

"Human will-power is the blind force which resists things, sometimes with seeming success, but only for a season.

"The great key-note to all right work is the attitude that 'I can of mine own self do nothing, but with God all things are possible.' At one bound we shift the responsibility of the situation on God, and He is abundantly able and equipped to put the enemy to flight.

"We do not struggle with the darkness in a room to get it out; we merely bring in the light, and the darkness disappears of its own self. Likewise with sin or sickness, or any material law, we do not need to fight it; we merely have to bring in the absolute truth that because man is made in the 'image and likeness of God' he is eternally protected and cared for."

The Woman Who Was Poor

MAZA was a widow who lived in a dirty little hut in the crowded quarter of Jerusalem. Each day she went into the temple and cleaned the great courts. But Maza was very poor and as she passed the coffers and saw her neighbors place certain sums therein she felt poorer than before, for she had not even the widow's mite to give, neither could she spare a crust of bread to anyone. And, further, she was unhappy because she had no friends. She had heard much of the Potter, Abd Allah, and how he had helped others to be freed from their burdens, and one night she determined to pay him a visit. So, after she had finished her work at the temple and eaten her meager meal, she turned her steps towards the dwelling of Abd Allah.

It was a wonderful night with a sky like a heavy blue vapor that seemed wholly to envelope the world. The moon had not yet risen and the stars were brilliant. But Maza saw none of the beauty; her eyes cast down, she trudged along wondering why her lot was so hard. So poor was she in spirit that she could not even lift her eyes to the heavens and feast her hungry soul on the beauty so lavishly displayed.

At last, after her long walk, she came to the lodging of Abd Allah and found him seated in the court, the boy Jethro playing on his harp

"Abd Allah," she called, with a note of distress in her voice; "I am burdened with poverty; wilt tell me of riches?"

Abd Allah arose and motioned Jethro to bring a small rug for her, on which he bade her be seated   They sat in silence for a while, and then Abd Allah began.

"There is no man in all Judea, be he ever so rich, and though he possess a palace of white marble, and slaves, and gold and silver in abundance, who has among his treasures a picture as magnificent as you have stretched before you at this moment, Maza." As he said this he pointed to the eastern skies where a blood-red moon was breaking through a rift in the long silver clouds. There was a telling silence as they all gazed in the direction he pointed

"First, then, Maza, always feast the soul, and this you can do as often as you will in the day or night, for the heavens cover all; and they are the great canvas of God; each day is a rare master-piece, designed and painted for you.   Then you are not poor because of the lack of beauty, for the whole world is overflowing with it."

"Go out into the sunshine, Maza, and lift your hands to high heaven and let your soul be filled with the blessed sunshine and blue sky   Let the oil of joy, the sheer joy of living, flow about you, and forget the material counterfeit of gold in your appreciation of the real gold of the sun   Let the sunlight of strength and trust in God dry up the stagnant morasses·of worry and care   Pour some of the dew of life eternal on your blasted

34

hopes and see them blossom forth into greater and nobler promises than before. Let the star dust light your way, instead of the dust of material ways cut off your vision of the stars."

Maza stirred a little; already she felt an uplifted thought, a stirring within, and Abd went on.

"There was once a certain woman who was very poor in thought and, in a state of desperation, she cried out for help, and the one who heard her cry was a man who understood the power of right thinking. He understood where the true source of supply was, he understood that God is mindful of His own, and that not a sparrow falleth without His knowledge, and he also understood how much greater are ye than many sparrows?' So he asked the woman, 'What have you in your house (mind)?' and the woman pondered a moment and said: 'Only a cruse of oil.' Now the man who understood knew the value of a cruse of oil (joy) and how a drop of it had saved many an axle from wearing away. So he said to her, 'Borrow vessels not a few.' So she borrowed vessels (made her thought receptive) Then the man started filling the vessels out of the cruse of oil, and presently they were all filled, and still the cruse (source) was not empty, for joy increaseth every time it is left to run loose, and a smile an inch long may stretch miles, yea! it may even encircle the globe. But this was not all that was to be done; now the activity was begun, it was necessary to continue to keep the joy moving, so he said to her: 'Go sell the oil' Action is the law of progress. It is necessary to give out joy and happiness and not stand with our vessels full meekly waiting for someone to come to us. Enter some darkened pathway where there is need of joy and scatter some light of good clean thinking as you go, and people will find that you are not only useful but an absolute necessity. There is the biggest market in the world for joy, and the fewest dealers in it of any known commodity. So this woman went her way and as she went she found a ready market for her oil.

"In the smiling mind there is no room for worry clouds, there is no accumulated, stale thinking or care, for the smiling attitude keeps them at arm's length; yea, it even puts them to flight. This smile is not a silly, simpering, facial contortion, but a strong, clean, healthy mental attitude that refuses to be downed by obstacles.

* * * *

"And it also happened that certain fishermen had labored all night (worked in ignorance) without success, and they were heavy hearted and discouraged, when the voice of Truth spoke to them and admonished them to cast their nets on the right side. Now, literally, to cast their nets on the right side would be casting them in the same waters they had fished all night, but they knew that to cast their nets on the right side was merely a command to change their thought from one of limitation to abundance, to know that God is good, and that 'He knoweth that ye have need of these things,' for is it not He that 'prepareth a table before me in the presence of mine enemies', in the presence of famine, want and woe? What wonder then, when they cast their thought into the inexhaustible source of supply, that their nets were full?

"Maza, supply is a law of God. He it is Who created you, and He is responsible for you. Has He not oft referred to you, in the sacred scrolls as 'His child?' Are not His promises kept? Did He not say, 'Seek and ye shall find. . . . ; ask and ye shall receive?' Is He that created you not able to sustain you, and that abundantly, too? Did He not say of man that he was created in 'the image and likeness?' You are His idea, perfect and eternal, and will He not keep you? Can the reflection manifest any condition that the original does not? and are you not a reflection of His love? It is good to know that you are living and moving and having your being in God; and if you are living in this great inexhaustible source of all good, can you want for anything? Rather I say unto you, reach out and take possession of your divine heritage. Open the doors of your thought so that the streams of Love can flow in and out of it."

And rising, Abd Allah continued: "Maza, what have you in your house?" and she answered him: "Gratitude and Love," and he said: "Go back to thy dwelling in peace and remember that Love freed is like bread cast upon the waters; it will return and nourish you when most needed."

And Maza went her way, a song of thanks in her heart and her soul full of the beauty of the night.

Jethro's Song

Just for today, dear weary heart,
Give up thy struggles; lean on me.
Forget all worry, come away,
Out where the silver brooklets play.
Out in the fields where daisies fair
Nod smilingly, without a care,
Where poppies greet thee with a flame,
And all the air breathes forth His name.
Amid green pastures let us stray
To seek and find the Perfect Day.

Where is the Perfect Day you seek?
Is it in valley, stream or hill?
Is it in city, mart or field?
Is it among the lilies fair,
That we shall lose all earthly care?
No, weary heart, it is not there,
So far away you need not go.
The Perfect Day is close at hand;
'Tis in the Consciousness of man.

Then, first, we look within the mind
And sweep it clean of thoughts that bind.
No room for worry, care and strife;
No place for evil, hate or rife.
No looking backward, just to see
The dark, dark road that used to be.
But open wide your thought and find
Flood-tides of love that fill your mind.

39

And once this mind is full of love,
A holy watchman from above
Shall guard the portals, day and night,
And put all evil care to flight.
And peace that passeth all shall be
Thy home for all eternity.
And He shall come and sup with thee—
And surely on thy upward way
Thy lips shall sing the Perfect Day.

The Power of Silence

ONE day when Abd Allah and Jethro were seated at their work, two men came along the way madly jesticulating and arguing. There was strife and hatred manifest in their voices, and revenge gleamed through their eyes when looking in through the open gate, they paused, seeing Abd Allah, then entered the court at his beckoning. But immediately upon entering they began arguing again, each at the same time trying to place his case before Abd Allah.

"Peace, peace, my brethren; why this dissension. Know ye not the power of silence?"

"No," said one of the two in a surly voice. "But we would," rejoined the other. They sat down on the rugs which Jethro spread for them, and waited for Abd Allah to speak.

"You, Hajah and Casper, are Christian men and have read much in the sacred scrolls, and well call to mind how it is written that the blessed Savior was laid to rest in the tomb, and that a massive stone was placed at its mouth and a guard put over it. Now what happened in the silence of the tomb? Jesus, the Christ, worked out the solution to the material lie called death; he proved it to be nothing but a belief, and something to be overcome. But note that he did this in the silence. In the silence he went back to the real cause of man and listened for the guiding voice of truth, listened for the Word, 'which spake and it was done.' Could he have heard this Word in the hubbub of material wrangling? Was not this the power of silence?

"To the mortal sense silence may seem death, yet how often is the ugly grub of thought changing form and working out his problem in silence, and at the appointed time he breaks the material law of limitation and floats off in a freedom before unknown.

"God pervades the silence, and it is only in the silence that we can hear the voice of the great Omnipotent Guide."

"But Abd Allah," interrupted one of the men. "How can we feel the Power of Silence in our own work?"

"By being still, by quieting the material senses, one after another, and withdrawing into the 'secret place of the Most High.' And after you have shut out every material clamoring you can then hear the 'still, small voice,' which says, 'Peace be still' to all that is unlike God, good. This 'still, small voice' was the voice that spoke 'and it was done,' and it is the voice which said 'Let there be light' (understanding), and mortal chaos and darkness faded away."

"But when I would enter the 'secret place of the Most High'," said Hajah, "a million little voices clamor for admittance, first one thing and then another, and I cannot enter the Silence of which you speak."

"It is good to remember," said Abd Allah. 'Behold I stand at the door and knock: if any man hear my voice, and open the door (of his mind), I will come in to him, and will sup with him, and he with me.' At the same time evil is knocking for admittance, the Christ is also standing waiting to be let in, to sup with you. Which will you admit? To which will you give the most power? Does not the very thought that Christ is standing there knocking put to flight all evil and sinful thoughts, for they cannot live in his pure presence?

"Then, brethren, before you argue and disagree about a question, and become angry and hate one another, just step into the closet of your consciousness and shut the door on all material voices and listen to this wonderful voice, which will guide you right.

"Don't squabble with yourself mentally and wear yourself out with your arguments, either audible or silent arguments, but be firm and know that God is the source of your intelligence, and that right must prevail. Then when you have received your guidance you can issue forth from your closet, clad with a newness of spirit and love and righteous judgment; for, my brethren, you only want what is absolutely right, and when you know that the law of right is ever operative, how can aught else come to pass?

"What is so impressive as silence, and what carries with it so much dignity? It is the very essence of self-control and authority, and what is more pitiful than a man overcome of his anger? The noisy breakers beat against the shores in vain, they only carry with them destruction; but the mighty silent depth of the ocean carries a fleet on its bosom.

" 'Be still and know that I am God,' be still and listen for the underlying melody that pervades all silence. It is the melody of life. It is the power that leads beside still waters and green pastures."

The House That Stood in Darkness

NOW it happened there lived, near the east gate of the city a nobleman, his wife, and their daughter, who was called Rhetta, because her skin was like the lily leaf turned to the morning dew, and her eyes were soft as the eyes of a fawn. And she was well beloved, this maiden Rhetta, and was daily found doing good deeds and bestowing kindnesses on those who were unhappy. But, the Last Enemy called at the palace one day and claimed as toll for his visit this lovely maiden.

All the country round about grieved for the fair Rhetta, and a great flower-laden procession followed her to her last resting place. The unhappy nobleman and his wife were as people without hope in the world and the marble palace was hung with black, and the doors and windows were shut. Moreover, in time, the lovely garden, wherein Rhetta was wont to spend many happy hours among the flowers and exquisite marbles that adorned it, became a weed patch. Thistles replaced the roses, and ugly wild vines clung to the marbles and strove to conceal their whiteness and beauty. It was the house desolate; it bespoke the futility of human existence; and from a thing of beauty it had become an eyesore.

Now in accordance with the custom in Jerusalem, the man and his wife spent their time on the roof of the house, which looked out over the city

on one side and towards wonderful Lebanon on
the other. June was at her height; wild flowers
made the hills and valleys riotous with color, en-
hanced by the brilliant butterflies fluttering from
flower to flower, and the birds darting and soar-
ing through the clear, transparent air, a song
streaming from their throats, "Come out and
live! live! live!" Everything called out to the
man and his wife to live and be happy. But so
deep were they sunk within themselves in their
sad thoughts that they heeded nothing.

And it was on this very day that Abd Allah and
Jethro were returning from the market where
they had been to sell the vases Abd had made, and
Abd Allah went on ahead, while Jethro followed
with the mule. He was playing a strange little
melody and setting words to it, to suit his fancy,
a melody with an appealing minor strain in it:

Life is a Circle which has no end,
Death does not break the link,
Death is but sleep.
Life is eternal, naught can be lost.

And the woman sitting in sadness, stirred on
hearing the strange music, and said to her husband, "What means this strange youth, saying
'Life is a circle which has no end'?" And her
husband, looking after them, said: " 'Tis Abd
Allah and his boy returning from the market He
is said to have a strange philosophy which has
explained away many of the cares of this life,
and he has put his philosophy into the mind of
this boy Jethro so that he sings it and accom-
panies himself on his harp."

46

"Would he could heal my broken heart," said the woman. So the man, rising, struck a brass gong and a black slave appeared "Master, at your service," he said, bowing low. "Go after the man and boy who have just passed, and bid them as my guests to rest a while with us"

* * * *

When Abd ascended to the roof the man, rising, said: "Greetings to thee, Abd Allah," and, bowing, he motioned him to a rug which the slave had spread for him. Jethro, who stood behind, was opened-eyed in wonderment. He it was who saw the exquisite white marbles hung with black, and the great flower urns standing empty at one side. Nor were the rich oriental rugs lost to his view. All the riches in the world are as naught without the proper mental attitude toward real substance.

The servant, moving noiselessly about, brought cigarettes and black coffee.

"We have heard your boy singing a strange song," the man said. 'Life is a circle—' What meaneth the youth?" And then, continuing, he said· "And what meaneth 'Death does not break the link'?" Abd made ready to reply, but the nobleman said further "Has not our beloved Rhetta been carried away by the Last Enemy, and taken from our sight?"

Then Abd Allah answered and said: "Believest thou in God, and that He is everywhere?"

"We believe in God and that He is good," they replied in unison.

47

"Knowest not that He is Life eternal, and that he is changeless? Then how can death happen in an infinity of life? Can God change, or one of His ideas pass into oblivion?"

A profound silence fell upon them as Abd Allah continued: "Life may change form; the tadpole in yon pool would not forever remain an insect, but he would enlarge his capabilities, and by changing form he becomes a frog, losing none of his former capacities, but attaining an advanced state of progress. Does the ugly grub die when it changes into a radiant butterfly, and is that which is left behind, either grub or butterfly? Would you have the beautiful butterfly, which had cut through the ugly cocoon and outgrown the narrow confines of the grub state, return to its former condition? And what other than a selfish motive could prompt your wishing its return? It is plain that it would not be good for the butterfly, neither would it make it happy, yet it might satisfy your selfish desire for possession. Then when our loved ones in their line of progress have burst into a freedom that we know not of, is it for their good and happiness that we wish them back, or is it to satisfy our selfishness?

"Is not then death, in its true meaning, progress? Is it not unfoldment? Does not the flower unfold at the expense of the falling away of the seed? Yet is the seed dead?

"Did not the Great Master prove that death was a myth, when he rolled away the stone from the tomb, which stone had seemingly set the seal on the reality of death? Did He not say: 'Our friend Lazarus sleepeth; but I go that I may awaken him out of sleep?' And then his great command, 'Loose him and let him go; free him from the winding sheets of mortal belief, which says that death is the end, that it is real and terrible, that it is the outcome of life Again I say unto you, Life is eternal.

"Can you conceive of God who is ever present, becoming inactive? God, good, is perpetual motion, and we, His perfect ideas and expressions of His thought, are controlled and governed by this perfect law of activity; then inaction or death can never occur, though the idea or expression may change form.

"Who, then, knowing this law of progress, will try to shackle it by wishing and sorrowing for those who have gone before and have cut through the shell of materialism? Does the mother grieve when her child lays aside his primer and takes the next book in hand? Rather does she not rejoice and say: 'He is progressing; knowledge and understanding are replacing ignorance. He is finding his way out of darkness, which is ignorance.'

"What is it that dies? Is it man, the 'image and likeness' of the Eternal God? Is it the perfect idea of God, which is sustained by Him, that dies? And whence comes a counter power to omnipotence which destroys the works of His mighty Hands?

"Are we paying the right tribute to those gone before when we hang our walls with black and sit mourning, forgetting to live and to reach out and help others, who are here with us? Is the garden yonder which is in weeds, a tribute to the loveliness of her whom you mourn? What fainting heart gazing thereon would take courage and new hope?

"So I say unto you, my good people, take from thy windows these dark hangings and throw wide open the doors and let in fresh air and sunshine, and set again the garden with roses, and watch the desert blossom.

"'I am the resurrection and the Life, though a man were dead (ignorant of true life) yet shall he live again.'

"Come, Jethro, sing for us."

I will say of the Lord
He is my refuge most High;
He is life eternal, and man cannot die.
Death is a dream, in Truth we awake
And every law of man will God surely break.

* * * *

As they again wended their way along the street, Jethro sang his song of "Life is a Circle," and the woman, lifting her eyes, smiled through tears and said "Life is a Circle, there is no death."

Love

ADGA, the beautiful, the adored, the well-beloved and idol of her father's heart, had just stepped from the white marble Roman bath, over which presided two statues of youth, supporting in their hands a lamp which cast the palest green tinge over the water and the marble fittings of the room. Her maids were massaging and anointing her with precious oils and perfumes of the orient, while a third black slave stood gently swaying a gorgeous fan.

In the midst of this oriental luxury, as she reclined on a long marble bench over which was thrown a rich piece of crimson stuff, she looked very much like a wonderful bit of marble, the masterpiece of some artist, which had been thus carelessly placed in this elaborate bath, save for her wonderful raven locks that in their blackness almost seemed to have a deep purple hidden in them, which fell over her white shoulders and back in great, thick ringlets. Her eyes were blue and steady in their gaze, edged about with long dark lashes, and were not unlike pools that one finds in the heart of some dense forest.

She had a lithe, slimly built body, rather of the sinuous type, and wholly unlike other maidens of her race. Her haughty, thin lips and finely chiseled features contrasted strangely with the full sensuous beauty of other maidens of the orient.

By an indulgent father she had been given the sobriquet of Adorée, by which name she was generally known. Being the only daughter of a wealthy nobleman, and a Christian, she had been indulged to an extent unheard of in that country. In fact she even had the companionship of men, and her father had left the choice of a husband to her own liking—a condition long since desired, but not yet attained in Jerusalem.

Of suitors Adorée had many, and from many lands, for her fame as a beauty had been sung abroad. They had acclaimed her the most beautiful woman of the orient, and had eulogized her in song and poetry as the "Midnight of a June Garden," "the Twilight of the Desert," "the Purple Mist of the Sunset." Her tiny white feet were spoken of as possessing the fleetness of the deer on the snow-capped mountain.

Now Adorée had listened to the songs of many lovers and had thrilled at their praises, but underlying it all she felt that there was an emptiness, and that their songs were called forth only by the physical; that when her beauty faded then the worship and love would cease, and possibly sooner. "Love was so fleeting a quality as this," so her old nurse had told her, and taught her the secrets of beauty, and admonished her to stay beautiful so that her lord and master might be pleased. But deep in the heart of Adorée there was a longing for something more substantial, something more enduring and stable; so one by one she sent her lovers on their way, and one by one they vowed to seek a watery grave or go into the desert and become a sun sacrifice.

Alas, this maiden who had all that material wealth could bring her, was unhappy, and she sighed as her maid clasped the heavy gold bands on her pretty white ankles.

"For what sigh you, oh, lovely Lady of the Midnight?" asked one of her maids. "You of all maidens are to be envied, for within your possession is power, beauty and riches; yea, and lovers by the score. What more could a maiden wish for?"

And Adorée, answering, said: "For love, Misma, for love," and, pushing back the heavy black ringlets, she took the golden head-band from the maid and adjusted it herself, using the green pool for her mirror "For love," she continued as if talking to herself; "that is not physical; for something more noble than the worship of body, wealth and jewels. Oh, Misma, is there no such love, is there nothing but the shifting transient sense of happiness?"

"My lady, thou art not well this day, or else thou art awry with some strange dream of the night What more could you wish for? Have you not the love of a hundred men, ready to do your bidding?"

"Yes, but I have not the love of one who knows that love is not consuming, but upbuilding and unfolding."

"You speak of the strange love that Abd Allah tells of at the East Gate, and there are many that believe in it, but for me, it is naught but talk."

"Who is Abd Allah," said Adorée.

"Do you not know the potter and letter writer named Abd Allah? He is said to lift a great burden from the shoulders of many by his happy philosophy."

"At eight bells tonight we shall go to him and hear what he has to say of love," said Adorée, rising.

"But, Lady Fair, we cannot go alone to this remote hut of the potter. It is by the north gate and the way is very dark and some say it is the way of beggars and thieves.

"Nevertheless," said Adorée, "we shall go. You shall accompany me, Misma "

*   *   *   *

The night dropped down like a heavy curtain, cutting off the beauty of the sunset with a thick mantle of clouds, but at the sounding of eight bells Adorée and Misma, robed in heavy travelers' cloaks, set out for the dwelling of Abd Allah.

A high wind had set in and the heavens became the playground of a million hideous cloud phantoms, which raced across the sky in mad terror.

"Let us turn back," said Misma. "It bids fair to be a terrific hurricane." But Adorée said, "We shall continue. It cannot be much farther for we can see the dark outline of the great wall."

Presently a reddish light flared up in the heavens, turned to blue and died down again, followed by a faint rumble of thunder, and again the maid spoke of returning: "Oh, my lady, shall we not take shelter and return home, and come again another night when it is not so terrible?"

"Misma," said Adorée, "this night is not more unquiet than my mind. I am weary and worried, seeking for happiness and true love."

* * * *

As they neared the court of Abd Allah's dwelling the storm was upon them. Great bolts of lightning utterly tore the heavens, to be followed by diabolical claps of thunder that were deafening, then by a silence that was almost tangible.

"Who goes there?" called Abd Allah as the women entered the court "What seek you at this hour and in this storm? Are not the gates of the city long since closed and all men safely in their homes?"

"I seek thee, Abd Allah," said Adorée. "And I have come to thee through this storm, which is much akin to my mental state, to know of a love that is not physical, to know of a love that does not deal with passion and that will not falter. Oh! Abd Allah, I am weary of this shifting, changing love Can you tell me of real love?"

Standing there before the doorway, the heavy cloak dropped from her shoulders, and by the flashes of lightning Abd Allah could see her wondrous beauty, and said: "Is this not the Lady Adorée, the praise of whose beauty is sung in a thousand ballads?" "Yes," she answered, "and I would know of love."

55

So Abd Allah, in his direct manner, bade them enter and placed rugs for them.

"God is Love, and since God is unchangeable, love must be likewise; and since God is everywhere Love must be everywhere. God is Life, and God is Love; then true Life is Love and is eternal, since Life is eternal. Love that is material is of few days and full of trouble; it builds upon a foundation of sand. It is elusive, for the moment you think you possess it, lo, it has slipped through your fingers and fluttered on to another. And, lastly, it is limited and does not belong to God; hence it cannot satisfy.

"Love then is universal and reaches out to all. It is active goodness, and is found seeking its 'own in another's good' Love is true service. It is the veiled figure which bestows its alms at night It is the helping hand that lifts the fallen and sets him on his feet again. It is the something in the mother's kiss that heals the wounded baby finger, and replaces tears with smiles It is the tender word spoken at the right moment; it is the sheer joy of living, of being happy and useful.

"Love is pure. It is the dove sipping the dew from the lily chalice. It is the blue that peeps through the dark clouds of material sense, and whispers that the storm is far spent. It is the thrill of joy that the shepherd knows when he finds the lost sheep. It is the something in the hand clasp of a long lost friend. It is the 'rod and staff' that both help and guide.

"Love is giving, not hard gold, but good thoughts, thereby helping the beggar to help himself return to his perfect estate.

"Love is the fulfilling of the law, and God is the law.

"Love is work in the Master's vineyard. Know ye not that the fields are white but the laborers (lovers) are few?

"Love is liberty, and by loving man aright we can liberate him from the bondage of material thinking We can set free all the slaves that we are holding in bondage in our thinking by loving them as the children of the Perfect One."

Now, as Abd Allah ceased speaking, a breathless silence fell upon them and each in his heart was praying the prayer of thanksgiving, for each felt the mantle of true love gently enfolding him.

And Adorée, rising, said· "Love was all about me, and all I had to do was to put my hand out and take it, yet I did not know it It was calling to me and beseeching me and yet I could not answer. But now I know what real love is, it is service; it is right thinking and consequent right living and doing; it is praising God, not with long prayers and speeches, but with silent voicings of gratitude and willingness."

And as they went their way the storm had spent itself and the deep blue of the night was beginning to peer through the clouds And so they returned through the dark by-ways clad in the white and shimmering robes of Love.

The Man Who Lost A Friend

OFTEN were they seen together, these two friends, Haaj and Absalom. Wrapped closely in the mantle of friendship they even excited envy and jealousy because of their nearness, because of the protection they afforded each other. They had been called Damon and Pythias, for they held each other above all else. But one day, into this haven of perfect friendship and love crept a serpent. At first they refused to listen for a moment to its insidious suggestions and arguments, but the serpent was not to be put aside thus easily; he was not destroyed, only cast aside, and he returned more subtle than before, and at length one of them yielded to the alluring voice of wrong, of jealousy and of envy, and turning against his friend, stabbed him to the heart. Not that he stabbed him with a knife of steel, but with a sword of hate, which cut deep and spilled the life blood of their friendship.

And one day he came to Abd Allah, this man who had been betrayed. He was dejected and downcast, for he had loved his friend well. And Abd Allah, looking up from his work, said:

"Greetings, Haaj; where is Absalom, for to see one of you is to see both." And Haaj, with sorrowful words, told the story of his lost friend, and said to Abd Allah:

59

"Abd Allah, thou knowest well that I laid upon him purple and fine linens, and threw about his neck a golden chain, and did show him preference in all things, and then, when one came and whispered in his ear suggestions of distrust, did he not run me through with the sword of hate and leave me by the wayside bleeding almost unto death from the wounds his cruel words and actions had inflicted, and leave my faith in man a shattered thing?"

And Abd Allah, rising, put his arm about Haaj and said· "Peace be unto you, Brother Haaj. Recall you not the First Law, 'Thou shalt have no other gods before me?' Were you not, in a measure, making your friend a god? Were you not setting him up as a something to be looked up to above all else, even defying his personality? Was it not for him that all the pearls of your thinking were saved? Then count it not a loss but a gain that the law of progress has forced you to 'lean not on your own understanding,' and further to put not your trust in the shifting, changeable material something called man, but to turn, first to God, Who is good, and Who is thy true friend.

Count him then not thy enemy, but thy friend for he has once again brought you into contact with God and restored you to rightful sonship.

"And if he has trampled your pearls under foot, does it not teach you to guard with greater care your pearls (thoughts) in the future and cast them not down again? They are precious and if any man seek them, be not slow in giving,

60

but do not force them, else the swinish desire in man will rend you In return for your pearls of love and good thinking, he would cast over your head jets of hate and deceit. These, I bid you, cast aside, for they are not worthy of aught else

"Look yonder at the dome of the Mosque of Omar. See how it stands out against the blood-red sunset. Is it not like a splendid white pearl in a glass of wine? Yea, like a stupendous reproduction of Cleopatra's glass of wine in which she tried to dissolve the last emblem of purity that she possessed, that she might consume it. That she might consume purity and scorch its white robes with the heat of the flesh pots of Egypt. But, as with Cleopatra, though purity and goodness were submerged in the wine, they were only hidden, and not destroyed, so with your love for your friend: it is only hidden in the maddening intoxication of the wine of mortal hate, and when he shall have drained the glass of its bitter contents and wallowed in the slime of his own mistake he will find this pearl, still unsoiled and untouched, and will prize it as the 'pearl of great price.'

"Not hate, but pity, is what should fill your heart, the pity the Master felt when he looked out across the sea of angry faces and lifted up his eyes and said: 'Forgive them for they know not what they do.'

"Love more; that is your keynote, not the selfish human love that desires to possess, but the love that liberates and makes free; and remember, 'I: I be lifted up (purified in thought), I shall draw all men unto me'

"Was it not said by the Master, 'When thy father and mother forsake thee I will take thee up?' Then can you want for a closer friend than He who marketh the sparrow's fall?

"Go feed among the lilies, Haaj; 'tis not your part to suffer because another has offended you. He is the one to suffer and will in proportion as you rise above the wrong he has done you; as you are superior to it, it will then find no abiding place in your thought and return to its source to destroy itself.

"Selfish human friendship is like a grain of mustard seed which is tightly grasped in the hand,—it cannot grow nor develop, and is worthless. The right kind of friendship is like a mustard seed which is planted in fertile soil,—it is constantly developing, and while it may be the joy of one, it is not shut out from others. As there is enough sunshine for all, so is there enough friendship and love for all."